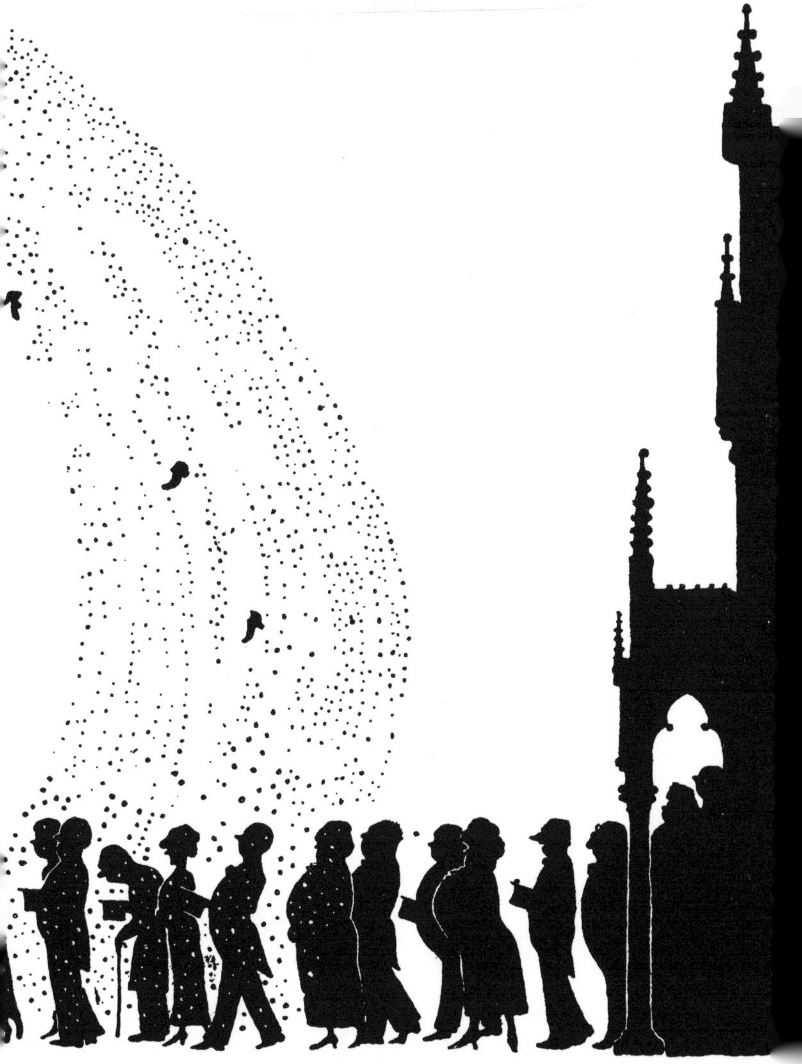

HOW TO BE A
PERFECT
HUSBAND

This edition first published in 2018 by the Bodleian Library
Broad Street
Oxford OX1 3BG

www.bodleianshop.co.uk

ISBN: 978 1 85124 490 4

First published in 1937 by Hutchinson & Co. Ltd.

Cover design by Dot Little at the Bodleian Library
Designed and typeset by Roderick Teasdale in
11.5pt on 11.5pt Tw Cen MT Light
Printed and bound on 90gsm Munken Cream by
TJ International Ltd., Padstow, Cornwall

British Library Catalogue in Publishing Data
A CIP record of this publication is available from the British Library

HOW TO BE A PERFECT HUSBAND

HEATH ROBINSON
and
K.R.G. BROWNE

Bodleian Library
UNIVERSITY OF OXFORD

DEDICATION

(a) With Respectful Sympathy To: The Newly-Married, the About-To-Be-Married, the Long-Married, the Ex-Married, the Frequently-Married, and even—such is our combined love for our fellow-creatures—People Who Would Not Marry If They Were Paid To Do So.

(b) With Sympathetic Respect To: The President, Vice-President, Chucker-Out, and Other Officials of the Probate, Divorce, and Admiralty Division.

W. HEATH ROBINSON.
K.R.G. BROWNE.

CONTENTS

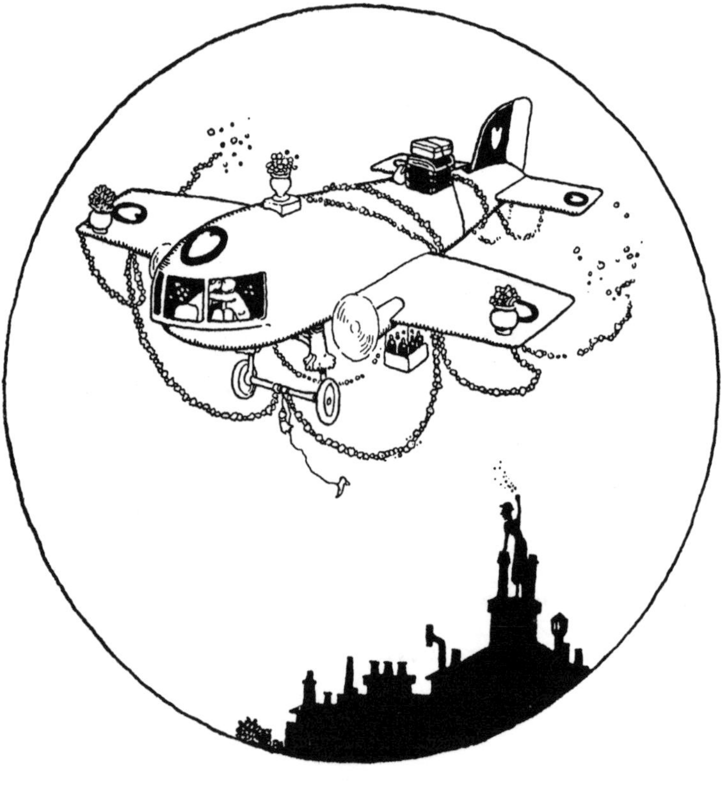

The air honeymoon

*What is Wrong with Marriage is almost invariably
the husband*

INTRODUCTION

As a topic for those who, having been dropped on their heads when young, write chatty articles for the daily papers, Marriage is probably the most popular on the market. It is a rare day—all *too* rare, in my opinion—on which nobody seizes quill and ink-horn and dashes off a snappy 1000 words on "What is Wrong with Marriage?"; "Marriage: Its Cause and Cure"; "Why is Marriage, Exactly?" or some other aspect of the marital state (as it is usually called by those who object on moral or political grounds to saying "marriage" twice in one paragraph).

It is noticeable, however, that most of these little homilies, or chunks of nonsense, have a strong feminine bias. (This is not, perhaps, surprising, as most of them are written by elderly unmarried ladies of the type that wear pince-nez attached to the left ear by a kind of miniature hawser.) One gathers, indeed, that when strife breaks out in the home and the air becomes thick with harsh words, recriminations, and (in extreme cases) crockery, the little woman is hardly ever to blame. It would appear, in short, that What is Wrong with Marriage is almost invariably the husband.

It is to remedy this state of affairs that Mr. Heath Robinson and I, in our impulsive, big-hearted way, have compiled this little text-book, which can also be used to press cowslips and/or swat moths. While we do not claim that the mere perusal of its fascinating pages will convert a confirmed bachelor into the sort of husband who wins Dunmow Flitches, we do feel that any young man who is contemplating matrimony for the first time might do a good deal worse than give it the once-over. And we might add—in fact, we *will* add, for who can stop us?—that as it contains nothing that could bring a blush to the most girlish cheek, matrimony-contemplaters of the other sex can learn quite a lot from it too.

It seems odd that it has been left to Mr. Heath Robinson and myself to perform this public service. Husbands first came into being a considerable time ago—long before the corkscrew and the celluloid collar—but nobody, so far as can be ascertained, has ever provided them with a handbook. The beginner who takes up, say, bee-keeping—doubtless because he has been crossed in love and wishes to forget—can walk into any bookshop that will allow him credit and acquire a variety of works on apiculture (as it is laughingly called, for some reason), ranging from *The Amateur Apiarist's Vade-Mecum*, by O.J. Corklady, to

The bee-keeping beginner

The Adventures of Queenie The Bee, by Emmeline Doolittle Stoop. By studying these during the long winter evenings he can learn all the rules of the game and acquaint himself with the eccentricities of his little pets before he buys a second-hand hive on the instalment-system and gets stung for the first time.

3

To date, no such assistance has been available to the novice husband. Hitherto the latter has had to get along as best he could by observing his father's behaviour at home and doing precisely the opposite. This is obviously a makeshift and unsatisfactory plan, because it is far harder to be a successful husband than to keep a bee happy and content. The mind of Woman

The mind of Woman works in mysterious ways

Buying a new wife in the Stone Age

works in mysterious ways and many a young husband has been flung out into the snow, with a rapidly swelling bump where the rolling-pin caught him, merely because he did not know his matrimonial onions.

There are those who say that the best method of maintaining harmony in the home is the "cave-man" or "treat-'em-rough", as practised by Henry VIII and other notables of the past.

As if she were a piece of genuine Sèvres

Singing about her daily tasks

But women are more exacting nowadays. In this year of grace and high income-tax, the husband who likes a quiet life must handle the sharer of his joys and overdraft as carefully as if she were a pedigree racing pigeon or a piece of genuine Sèvres.

An error at the start of his married life

This is no simple job, because wives differ from racing pigeons in being easily affronted, and the novice husband is very apt to commit some error at the start of his married life which will subsequently make him wish that he had never been born at all.

Hence this little, but—in our opinion—not uncomely, book. In placing it reverently before the great, bat-headed, about-to-be-married public, Mr. Heath Robinson and I are inspired purely by a desire to help our fellow men. (To those who are past help we offer our deepest sympathy, with the reminder that a hundred years from now nothing will matter very much.)

As to our qualifications, we can only say that we have both been married, more or less successfully, for more years than our wives care to have mentioned in public. As an additional proof of our altruism, we had intended to publish, as a frontispiece, our photographs, which we feel could hardly fail to convince the most sceptical reader of our disinterestedness; but the publishers, for reasons which they decline to state, do not see eye to eye with us in this.

So there it is, wherever that may be. It only remains to add that we hope a good time will be had by all, and that nobody will blame us if it isn't.

A toss-up

SELECTION OF A MATE

In as much as it takes two to make a quarrel and/or a marriage, the would-be husband's first step towards attaining his ambition must obviously be the selection of a mate. This is a matter calling for the greatest care, as there is nothing more awkward about the house than an ill-chosen wife.

Refraining, then, from proposing to the first wench who throws him a beckoning glance, the beginner should decide what *type* of wife he needs. Of girls, as of gin, gooseberries, and gas-meters, there are several varieties—among others, the Sporting, the Studious, the Athletic, the Beautiful, the Thick-Ankled, and the Completely Dumb. (From one point of view, the last-named make the most satisfactory wives, being solid ivory from the neck up and consequently ready to believe anything; but as companions for a lifetime they are not so hot.)

10

SELECTION OF A MATE

The young man who craves the kind of married life that involves the daily exchange of personal abuse and even small china ornaments has only to marry a girl of the wrong type. Thus, a youth who is keen on golf—which means that he has neither the time nor the intelligence to be keen on anything else—would be well advised to keep away from dames who understand Einstein's Theory and can make the Binomial Theorem do everything but play the zither. Conversely, a young man whose favourite bed-book is Dr. Schmell's *The Relation of Interplanetary Ratiocination to Anti-Chimerical Subversives* is no soul-mate for a little duck who believes that it was Nelson who exclaimed: "Up, Guards, and drat 'em!" after losing a leg at the Battle of Prestonpans.

The carnivorous male who woos a she-vegetarian is simultaneously courting big trouble, as is the ardent poetaster who makes overtures to one of those

Who woos a she-vegetarian ...

Can she darn a sock?

weather-beaten females who thunder about hockey-fields on large, flat feet, standing no nonsense whatever. In other words, incompatibility of temperament—as it is laughingly termed in the Divorce Court—is the rock on which many a frail matrimonial bark has foundered with both hands. (Applications for the dramatic, gramophone, and lampshade rights in the above simile should be made to the publishers. No reasonable offer refused.)

Moreover, even when a potential bride of the right type has been found, the wise suitor will not commit himself in any way—and, above all, not in writing—until he has examined her character in detail and found no grievous flaws. Can she, for example, cook? What are her views on spinach, Marx (Karl), the Liberal Party, oysters, Equality of the Sexes, Ibsen's plays, hot-water-bottles, the nationalization of the coal industry, the works of Mr. Epstein, cricket for girls, round games, Marx (Groucho), the fiscal situation in Siam, and similar vital matters?

Is she addicted to (a) small woolly dogs that yap; (b) early rising; or (c) false eyelashes? When offered a marshmallow, does she giggle and say "Ta!" or decline with dignity and turn away? What are her reactions to the Albert Memorial? Can she darn a sock? Are her

What are her reactions to the Albert Memorial?

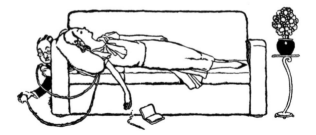

*Surreptitiously taking the blood pressure
of a possible fiancée*

table-manners above reproach? Is she a moderate eater, or is she likely to outgrow her mother, impossible though that may seem at the moment? Is she emotional in a scene-creating way, or can she be kept more or less in her place?

Not until he has satisfied himself on these and similar points should the husband-in-embryo allow the first cautious reference to orange-blossom to creep into the conversation. Generally the essential information can be elicited by tactful questioning, but there are a few simple tests to which every young girl should be subjected by her intending groom.

Par example (as the French say, knowing the language, as they dashed well ought to), to ascertain whether she flies too readily off the handle in times of domestic crisis—as when the geyser bursts, slaying several, or the fourth cook in three days beats it to pastures new—it is only necessary to take her to the movies and there sound her with a stethoscope borrowed from a medical friend. Should she bat no

Cautious youth sounding lady friend by stealth before making matrimonial proposal

eyelid during the most harrowing scenes, but continue placidly to munch her nougat, she may be assumed to have a pretty phlegmatic temperament. If, on the other hand, the stethoscope reports extreme agitation within whenever somebody plugs a sheriff or gets trapped in an airtight safe, her escort can be fairly sure that there will be moments in his married life when he will have to duck behind the sofa. In neither case, I'll bet a ducat, will he refrain from proposing, the poor sap!

A well-balanced carriage is to be looked for

Though love is notoriously blind, as a quick glance round our married acquaintances will show, the normal husband naturally prefers a wife at whom horses will not shy in passing. A well-balanced carriage, a figure that is neither so meagre as to be swayed by the lightest breeze nor so ample as to get jammed in doorways, a face which, while possibly incapable of launching even a hundred ships, can be relied on to scare no children—these are highly desirable qualities in a female helpmeet. There is nothing, of course, that a young man can do about his fiancée's face;

16

and, anyway, modern beauty-preparations can work wonders with the most unpromising materials. (Why, look at Mrs. ———. No, better not, perhaps.) But on the first two points he can easily satisfy himself with the help of a plumbline—see illustration—and the Heath Robinson "Ladyewaye" attachment for arm-chairs.

This latter apparatus, as the diagram shows, is quite simple in design, perfectly painless, and can be fitted to any bachelor's apartment. By its aid any young woman about whose tonnage there is a doubt can be weighed accurately, swiftly, silently, and so secretly

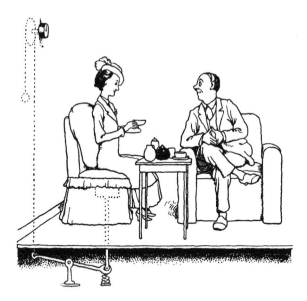

Inoffensive method of ascertaining the weight of a lady friend

Testing a new fiancé

that her enjoyment of the macaroons and cocoa is not even interrupted. I predict for this ingenious gadget a wide sale among smallish men who have no wish to be outweighed at all points by their wives.

Many a respectable young woman has been deterred from accepting the man of her dreams by the fear that he has leanings towards Gay Young Sparkiness. A husband who prefers gin-fizzes to geology, and who would rather spend an evening in a night-club than a week in the British Museum, is obviously no partner for a woman of quiet tastes and studious habits. And it was while taking a bath one morning last July that Mr. Heath Robinson conceived and worked out the Milk-and-Cocktail Test for damsels in doubt on this important matter.

When the young man calls, a little refreshment must be placed conveniently to his elbow. Milk—or a Manhattan: that is the question. If he reaches for the cocktail-shaker and drains it at a draught, he may as well abandon all idea of matrimony—since, alas, there can be no other girl for him—and become a hermit. But if he is found wearing a slightly shocked expression, with a half-empty glass of milk beside him, he can get busy with his wooing right away. And good luck to him, the estimable little fellow!

Ah, well! Neither Mr. Heath Robinson nor myself, tough old cynics that we are—though kind to animals and courteous to the aged poor—expect that the least attention will be paid to the foregoing suggestions by any bridegroom-in-embryo. It is the way of Youth, when struck by Cupid's dart, to go all soft and dewy-eyed, while simultaneously breaking out in coloured socks and evincing a deplorable tendency to write sonnets;

and it is almost impossible to do all these things and preserve a balanced mind. In other words, people will doggedly continue to marry the most unsuitable other people, and nothing we can do will save them.

Still, they can't say we didn't warn 'em.

Scoring a bull's-eye

For shuffling dominoes

COURTSHIP AND PROPOSAL

Having chosen, with or without our assistance, the future sharer of his joys, sorrows, overdraft, and maisonette (ring lower bell), the would-be husband is faced with the task of winning his lady's affection. Peacocks do this, they tell me, by spreading their tails and walking up and down a good deal; but the ordinary man, less fortunate in his plumage, must adopt other methods. One cannot, I mean to say, impress a modern girl by walking round and round her in a bowler.

The first and obvious step is to ascertain her interests, and chip in. Is she, for example, keen on halma? Then her suitor must just set his teeth and be keen on halma too; it will not hurt much, once the first pangs are over. Are (or is) dominoes her passion? Then let him cultivate a taste for this bizarre pastime

21

and pit his wits against hers in a nightly game. (The wise wit-pitter, however, will be careful to let her win at least five games out of seven, as otherwise she may turn fretful and flounce out, never to return.) As a token of his enthusiasm for her hobby, he might do worse than give her a Heath Robinson Domino-Shuffler, which can be constructed in a few moments from a second-hand egg-whisk and those portions of a sewing-machine which most easily unscrew.

Is she an ardent swimmer, counting that day wasted on which she does not astound the onlookers with her skilful trudgeon? Then he must conquer his natural distaste for water in any form, master the rudiments of the breast-stroke, and flounder manfully beside her. (By the way, may I draw the attention of all to the Heath Robinson Bathing-Suit for Evening Wear, designed for formal aquatic occasions? Though we cannot hope to outshine the peacock, we can at least look pretty snappy as we stand poised at the water's edge, bronzed and fit and the cynosure of all eyes.)

Another good way of attracting a woman's interest is to give her things—pearls, small yachts, two-seaters, mink coats, and the like. The youth who cannot afford such gestures can try his luck with packets of cigarettes or bunches of cow-parsley; but naturally he will not get such quick results. As for the swain whose means will not permit him to lay even a bag of acid-drops at the feet of his adored, I can only advise him to take her for a series of moonlight walks. True, the British moon is seldom there when needed for this purpose, while in recent years it has been greatly over-advertised by dance-band vocalists with their mouths full (apparently) of suet; but the pale orb of night

Gent's bathing-suit for evening wear

An object-lesson from Nature on domesticity

(copyright in all countries, including that little pinkish bit between Siam and China) can still be blamed for a good many announcements in *The Times*.

The power of suggestion, again, may usefully be brought into play by young males too bashful to mention Love without going mauve in the face. A country walk in Springtime, when all Nature smiles, and birds in their little nests are agreeing away like blazes, affords many charming object-lessons in the art of courtship. There is no prettier spectacle, to my mind, than a wooed young butterfly going all coy and whimsy; while a brace of mottled pie-finches—or a couple of cloth-eared nutlarks, if you prefer them—who have reached the question-popping stage are a sight to turn the dumbest

Another of Nature's little hints

maiden's fancy to thoughts of rice, old boots, etc. Ah, me! What it is to be young!

Ah, yes, but (the anxious young may inquire, fumbling with its hat) how is a man to know if his sentiments are reciprocated? The modern girl wears no heart upon her sleeve—if, indeed, she has a heart, which some think doubtful—and no man likes to propose unless he has a reasonable hope of hearing a softly whispered "Yes!" rather than a scornful "Nerts!"

Nature's hint

Well, to the experienced eye, even a modern girl reveals when her young heart has been ensnared. If, when Somebody enters the room, she starts as if stung by a hornet and goes all puce about the ears, it is a safe bet either that she is in a highly nervous state and needs medical attention, or that wedding-bells will soon ring out o'er marsh and fen and lea. And if information reaches him that in his absence she just moons about the house, all foggy-eyed and dreamy, dropping things repeatedly and tripping over mats, her admirer can safely clear his embarrassed throat and ask her to name the day.

Equalization

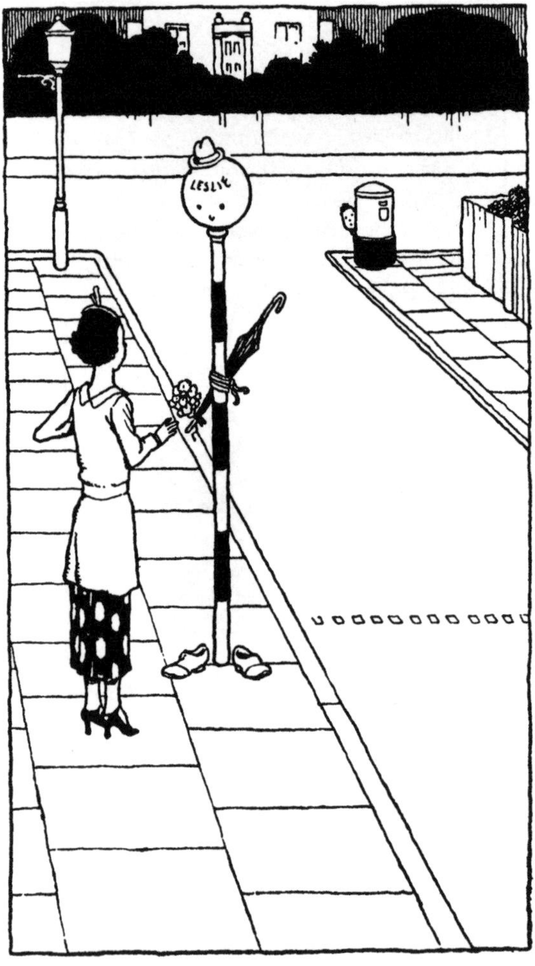
LESLIE

A bashful tribute

COURTSHIP AND PROPOSAL

Personally, I hold that the Tapioca Test is as good a method as any of deciding this vital question. The young man has only to take the girl out to dinner and at the appropriate moment offer her tapioca. The girl, naturally, will refuse with a delicate shudder, whereupon her cavalier should observe casually: "No? Now, I could never marry a girl who didn't like tapioca." This is the crucial moment, for if the wench replies: "Oh, yeah?" and asks for a banana, it is clear that she is still heart-whole and fancy-free. If, however, she hesitates for about three seconds, and then says shyly: "On second thoughts, Mr. Dumbell, I think I *will* have some tapioca. It's so delightfully vitaminous, isn't it?" then her companion can fling up his hat and rejoice, for he has found True Love at last.

As to the actual manner of the proposal, this has changed considerably in the past hundred years. In the Victorian age, when men's features lurked unsuspected behind a zareba of whisker, and the bustle was more of a garment than a habit, it took the form of a lengthy oration, delivered usually from the knees and prefaced by a gift of hollyhocks—or whatever flower it is that signifies to the initiated: "I'm that way about you, Baby." Beginning: "Miss Throttlebutt, you cannot, I venture to believe, be wholly insensible of the nature of the sentiments I have long entertained towards you . . ." and ending, rather hoarsely: ". . . so let me implore you, dear Miss Throttlebutt—dare I call you Susan?—to put an end to my suspense and make me the happiest man in England—nay, in all Europe!—by bestowing upon me the inexpressible honour of your hand in marriage", it lasted a full twenty-five minutes and did no good to the knees of the trousers.

But things are very different today. The modern suitor cannot absent himself from his office long enough to do the thing in the grand Victorian manner, while no modern girl can sit motionless and mum-chance for more than five minutes at a time. The modern proposal, therefore, is a brisk and business-like affair, averaging little more than a minute and a half from question-pop to troth-plight.

The direct method of attack, of course, is still the best: "Marry me?" "Yup." Many young men, however, are compelled by circumstances, shyness, or an impediment in their speech to approach the subject in a more round-about manner; and it is for the benefit of such that Mr. Heath Robinson—as kindly a man as ever refrained from kicking a stray cat—has devised and illustrated divers methods whereby tongue-tied swains (though not necessarily divers; dentists, deans, and even dukes will find them useful, too) can convey to the Only Girl in the World that they are simply cuckoo about her.

The shy young swain who is afflicted with premature baldness—as a result of worrying about his falling hair, or possibly because he has been gnawed about the head by mice—will find that the name of his adored, stencilled in some gay colour and surrounded by a conventional heart, makes an effective cranial decoration and can hardly fail, when paraded slowly back and forth beneath the lady's window, to give her a rough idea of what it is all about. If she is a quick-witted girl she will then respond, either by shutting the window with a bang (which means: "NO!"), or by beckoning smilingly, or smiling beckoningly (which means: "YES!").

An unobtrusive declaration

A mirror proposal

It may be as well to add that this method should not be employed in mid-winter by those who are subject to colds in the head, and that it is practicable only in the case of girls whose names are pretty terse. The youth who is enamoured of an Ermyntrude, a Persephone, a Claribel, or a Dulcibella must stifle his disappointment—

unless, of course, his is an exceptionally large head, owing to vainglory—and try something else, such as the Proposal by Reflection.

This, as the illustration shows, was designed primarily for the use of loving hearts that are continually being sundered by parental opposition; and like the Vanishing Lady illusion, it is all done by mirrors. The most ardent suitor finds it difficult to concentrate on his work when he knows that at any moment he may be hurled out into the night by an unfriendly father; but with the help of a stout wall and his mother's dressing-table mirror he can let himself go on the subject of bridesmaids, banns, and even bassinettes, and remain quite unkicked in the pants. That done, the elopement can proceed as planned.

It is also possible (see diagram) to propose under water, a nosegay of fragrant seaweed being substituted for the customary bouquet. This expedient is not recommended, however, to young couples whose circulation is poor or who dislike being pecked about the ankles by inquisitive denizens of the deep.

For all-round, everyday purposes the Proposal by Telephone is possibly the best, as it enables the suitor to pour out his soul at the very reasonable rate of two-pence for three minutes; while the knowledge that no hostile parent can get him with a horsewhip—which differs from a sheepwhip in being smaller in the middle and having deeper flanges—lends him additional assurance. Swains using this method, however, should ascertain that they have the right number *before* they declare their love. A friend of mine who omitted this precaution once found himself proposing to the Upper Tootham Home of Rest for Indigent Gentlewomen; and was his face red!

Well, that is about all, I think, that can usefully be said on this subject. Encouraged and fortified by the suggestions here set forth, any young man of marriageable age should now be able (a) to woo and (b) to win the object of his affections—always providing, of course, she prefers nobody else. Should an uncompromising rebuff be his unhappy portion, I would urge him to bite the bullet, have a soothing cup of tea, and remember that there are as good eels in the ocean as ever came out of it.

Unsuspected

*A judicious arrangement of duplicated
wedding presents*

THE WEDDING

The lady having murmured a shy "Yes" and consented to name the day—which, by the way, should never be April 1st, as to be wedlocked on that date is to become the butt of doubtful witticisms—the preparations for the nuptials must be put in hand. The precise character of the wedding depends on the inclinations and financial status of the contracting parties, some preferring to be spliced in the grand manner, with a gaggle of bridesmaids, a clutch of police, and a scuttle of hired waiters; and others electing to get hitched with the minimum of orchids and photography. In planning a wedding, as in buying a piano, you takes (so to speak) your choice and you pays (as it were) your money.

The bridegroom, naturally, has little or no say in this matter. His not to reason why; his not to protest

A much-appreciated gift: a super-de-luxe coffee-maker

that he looks awful in striped trousers and would prefer a quiet, almost furtive, ceremony, ungoggled-at by rubberneck relations; his but to stand about in corners, grinning sheepishly and fingering his tie, while the doings are organized by his future mother-in-law.

Once the date of the wedding has been announced in the Press, the presents will start trickling—or, with luck, pouring—in; and among them there should be at least one from the bridegroom to the bride, and vice versa. The majority of bridegrooms show all too little originality, in my opinion, in their selection of these gifts, their usual choice being a short hawser of pearls, a garnet-and-carbuncle brooch, or some such conventional gewgaw, expensive to insure and of no practical use. Pleasing though such gifts may be to a certain type of woman, there must be many who would appreciate something less stereotyped and more useful. The Heath Robinson Doublepiano, for example, makes a charming present for a musically minded bride and enables the young couple to play "The Sailor's Farewell to His Horse" and other popular duets without crowding each other off the piano-stool. For the young wife who cannot distinguish a semi-quaver from a bar of soap, may I suggest the Heath Robinson Two-Candlepower Coffee-maker? This machine is guaranteed to add distinction to any breakfast-table, and may work admirably, for all I know.

The doublepiano for married couples, to avoid cramping and friction when playing duets

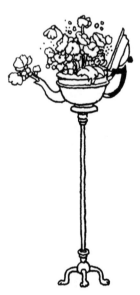

As to the other presents—the fish-knives, the embroidered egg-cosies, the sets of Tennyson in limp morocco, and the rest—these should be graded in their respective classes (i.e. the Fairly Useful, the White-Elephantine, and the Frankly Ghastly) and later disposed of accordingly. A few, in all probability, can be pawned for modest sums, and others ear-marked as Christmas presents for relatives who are too poor to take offence; while others, again—see accompanying diagrams—can be converted into something else and so made to earn their keep.

Thus, a superfluous coal-scuttle can readily be adapted to accommodate a smallish baby; unwanted teapots can be put to a variety of uses, from housing rare blooms to ornamenting mantelshelves; and even a hot-water-bottle, intelligently treated, can be made to start life anew as a more-or-less-modish toque.

Converted wedding presents

Training the bride's train-bearers

Regarding the ceremony proper—a ceremony of any other kind would not be tolerated for a moment, naturally—this, as I have said, can be either loud and lengthy, or brief and businesslike. Where bridesmaids and pages are employed, however, they should be thoroughly coached in their duties, as nothing is more disconcerting to a shy young bride than to be jerked flat on her back by a misjudgment of distance and/or stresses on the part of her train-bearers.

Though the practice of pelting newly married couples with rice and disused footwear is becoming obsolete—and not a moment too soon, inasmuch as hurriedly flung rice is apt to sting like blazes, while more than one frail bridegroom has been knocked senseless

40

by a well-aimed boot—confetti is still thrown a good deal at weddings of all sorts. A confetti-gun, as here depicted, is useful on such occasions, as it enables the keen confetti-thrower to discharge about four times the usual amount of ammunition with about five times the usual force, and so ensures that the young couple will spend the first evening of their married life in extracting the stuff from their ears.

*The new honeymoon car, fitted with
neat confetti plough*

41

The confetti-gun

The custom of stationing a guard of honour, armed with anything from saucepans or sabres to hockey-sticks or firemen's hoses, at the exit from the church, harms nobody and lends a touch of colour to the proceedings. The implements used in this quaint old rite should be of an appropriate character—e.g. an

THE WEDDING

The double veil to give protection from confetti

archway of dustbin-lids for a dustman and his mate, or an array of flower-decked averages for the bride of an average-adjuster.

With the knot securely tied, and the bride happy in the knowledge that she has bagged her man at last, it is customary at most weddings for all to attend a reception given by the bride's parents. These functions vary from the Large and Formal, with real champagne on sale-or-return and a detective in ill-fitting morning dress to keep an eye on the apostle spoons, to the Small and Matey, where the guests sit on the floor and eat rock-cake, etc. (There is also the Mildly Cranky, where all concerned are vegetarians

*An appropriate guard of honour at the
wedding of a domestic couple*

Drinking the bride's health at a homoeopathic wedding

or teetotallers or anti-vivisectionists, and stage their revels accordingly; but these are in the minority and need not concern us now.)

In recent years the old-style wedding-feast, where the company assembles round a groaning board and eats until its eyes bulge, has rather declined in favour—possibly because enthusiastic trencherwork is considered slightly vulgar in this diet-ridden age. Personally, I deplore this, because as a foundation for a contented married life a square meal has much to commend it. As any Harley Street physician will testify for three guineas, one can face the future far more confidently on a steak-and-kidney pie and a double portion of jam-roll than on a pint of dry Martini and a couple of stuffed olives.

HOW TO BE A PERFECT HUSBAND

To encourage a nation-wide renaissance of the wedding-breakfast habit, Mr. Heath Robinson has designed a typical lay-out for nine persons, a wren's-eye view of which is appended. (All the characters in this drawing are fictitious, no reference being intended to any living bridegroom, cat, or plate of dumplings.) The suggested viands have been carefully chosen to provide that happy blend of calories and vitamins which enable the digestion to do its stuff with hardly any discomfort to its owner; but the menu, naturally, can be adapted to suit individual tastes. Those, for instance, in whom haggis invariably induces hiccoughs can be regaled with a less eruptive dish, such as boiled ptarmigan on artificial toast or newts'-tongues fried in aspic. Broadly speaking, however, the simpler the food the shorter the meal, the briefer the speeches, and the sooner the guests can remove their boots and enjoy a little well-earned shut-eye.

Re speeches—if speeches there must be. Unless there are those among the guests who can only be deterred by laudanum or some blunt instrument from saying a few words, two speeches should suffice at any wedding—one from the bride's father, proposing the health of the young couple and containing at least one joke about two Irishmen (Pat and Mike), and a sheepish rejoinder from the bridegroom, replete with such clichés as "happiest day of my life", "undeserved good fortune", "luckiest man in England", and so forth. That done, and the necessary toasts having been honoured in tea, stout, or elderberry wine, the party can disperse in good order, providing nothing remains to be eaten.

So ends this red-letter day in the life of the happy pair. It only remains now for them to kiss everybody

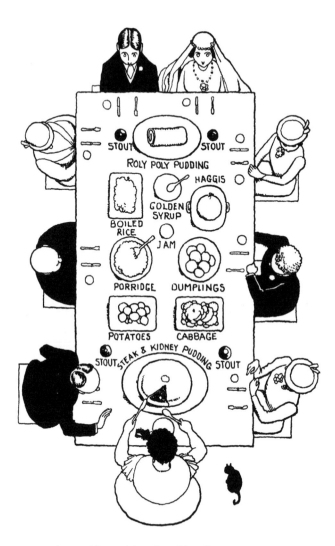

A sensible wedding breakfast for nine persons

good-bye, cry a little, change their clothes, climb into their barouche or limousine—to which a neat confetti-plough, designed to expedite their getaway, can be fitted at a small extra cost (see page 41)—and launch their little matrimonial bark upon Life's stormy sea.

And here's hoping it will keep reasonably fine for them, the sweet young things!

Bridegroom practising reply to wedding toast

Novelty in home millinery

EARLY MARRIED LIFE

As every lion-tamer knows, the King of Beasts cannot be expected to jump through paper hoops without a little preliminary tuition; and what applies to lions applies equally to wives. It is during the early days of his married life—when the honeymoon is but a fragrant memory and every pawnable wedding present has gone to its new home—that the wise husband will train his wife in the way that she should go—not so much with curses as by the power of suggestion and example. Once a woman gets set in her ways, it is practically impossible to pry her loose without the help of gun-cotton; and it is therefore up to her husband to see that she steps off, so to speak, on the right foot.

The most important of a wife's duties is, of course, the supervision of the culinary department—or "kitchen", as it is technically termed. In households where expense is no object, thanks to a bequest from a rich uncle or a lucky investment in an Irish Sweep, the actual dirty work is usually done by a gaggle of assorted serfs, churls, scullions, etc. Nevertheless, it is essential that the housewife should at least know how to boil an egg, as otherwise starvation will stare the family in the face whenever a strike or an epidemic of mumps breaks out in the basement.

The young husband, therefore, should assist the little woman to master the elements of cookery, either by standing her a course of training or by giving her a few tips himself. (Banana-frittering by the Heath Robinson method, for example, is seldom taught in schools, for some reason.) At the same time he should acquaint her with his own personal preferences in the matter of victuals, and give her a list of those dishes—e.g. tapioca, spinach, homemade seed-cake, cold stewed fish, and so forth—which have only to appear on the table to make him bubble at the eyes with rage.

More than one marriage has gone up in a cloud of smoke owing to the wife's inability to understand that an occasional night out with the boys is what every husband needs to preserve his reason and keep him from brooding on his care-free past. In the life of every man above the rank of moron there are times when the urge to go mildly gay in exclusively masculine company becomes too strong to be withstood; and it is by her behaviour at such moments that the young wife proves herself.

If, when her spouse timidly applies for the necessary leave, she at once assumes that his love is dead and scampers weeping to her mother, she may be held to have failed at her job. If, on the other

Demonstrating to the wife
a new method of frittering
a banana by electricity

*How to go to bed without disturbing
the household after a late night*

hand, she acquiesces smilingly and allows him an extra shilling from his wages for buns, lemonade, etc., she can be accounted not only a good wife, but a highly unusual one.

The husband who knows what is good for him will take pains to make this point very clear to his little old haybag—as he calls her affectionately—almost before he has scooped the last of the confetti from his ears. In return, the least he can do is to promise to remove his boots in the hall when he comes home, singing slightly, from his refined carousals, or to hoist himself silently to bed by an ingenious apparatus (here illustrated) which can be erected in a few moments by any reliable carpenter. It is on this basis of mutual give-and-take that all the most successful marriages, such as that of—er—such as that of—well, all the most successful marriages are founded.

There are, of course, certain minor matters in which every young wife needs a little kindly instruction. She must be taught, for one thing, that the correct way to squeeze a tube of tooth-paste is upwards from the bottom, *not* sideways from the middle. She must learn also that as a protection for carpets against the ravages of moths there is nothing cheaper or more effective than cigarette-ash. And lastly, she should be trained to exhibit no temperament when her soul-mate brings home unexpected guests to dine—or when they have gone, for that matter.

Yes, but—as some lady in black bombazine and a bonnet with bugles will almost certainly demand—what about the husband, hey? Does *he* contribute nothing to the success or failure of the deal? Is his life to be roses, roses all the way, while his wife turns somersaults at his

Crooning keeps alive the spirit of romance

command and wears her pretty fingers to the bone to keep him neatly underclothed and socked?

Not by a long shot, lady. As I have already implied, give-and-take is the thing that matters, and the wise husband knows that he, too, must play his part if his home-life is not to degenerate into a species of running dog-fight. There are many little ways in which, without unduly exerting himself or missing his nightly mug of buttermilk at the "Archdeacon's Arms", he can make himself useful about the house and earn a reputation for thoughtfulness that will stand him in good stead whenever he wishes to touch his mother-in-law for a fiver.

Peeling onions is one of several domestic duties which any woman will gladly delegate to anybody who cares to take it on. Few men are born onion-peelers, the majority being designed rather for the manipulation of corkscrews, but with the help of an arrangement of mirrors (see diagram) this sad-making task can be carried out with the minimum of inconvenience to the tear-ducts.

How to avoid tears when peeling onions

Again, experiment has shown that many lengthy husbands make admirable emergency clothes-props. As the illustration bears witness, a man of normal physique looks more than usually dignified at the end of a clothes-line, the more so as he can use the opportunity to study some improving book, from which informative extracts can be read aloud to the little woman as she pegs out the winter woollies. Husbands who suffer with their feet, however, should not volunteer for clothes-line duty more than once a fortnight.

Anyone can make a vacuum cleaner

A perfect husband is a prop to the household

In homes where the finances will not run to a vacuum cleaner, the husband who wishes to win an approving nod can either seize the dustpan and brush and do the job himself, thereby imposing a grave strain on his braces, or—if he is an indifferent stooper and of a mechanical turn of mind—devise an efficient substitute from the following simple ingredients, most of which will be found lying about in the attic: a disused saucepan, the bag part of a bagpipe, two-thirds of a chair, two short lengths of stove-pipe, a little horse-blanket, some stout twine, and divers portions of an old iron bedstead. With these, as the diagram explains, he can construct a vacuum-cleaner that will evoke gasps of admiration from the neighbours and swallow anything from a smallish Pekingese downwards.

In the same way, he need neither overwork his wife by commanding her to press his trousers—a job no woman is really keen on, or even good at—nor pawn the family plate to acquire a trouser-press. All he needs to preserve that knife-like crease which is the hall-mark of the snappy dresser is a garden-roller and a fine afternoon, the first of which can usually be borrowed, while the latter is bound to occur eventually. Many self-made men attribute their success to their lifelong habit of pressing their trousers in this manner and investing the money saved in sound Government stocks.

Newly married couple folding linen

*The perfect husband invariably presses
his own trousers*

The above-mentioned are but a few of the dodges
whereby the thoughtful husband can endear himself
to his wife and get himself pointed out in church as
a model Benedict. ("So helpful about the house, my
dear.") Many other little attentions—such as installing
a Heath Robinson "Lettasleep Roofalarm", being ever

How to prevent the alarum from disturbing the wife in the morning

Helping with the jumper

ready to wind wool with the help of a Heath Robinson "Eziwynda", and carrying always about his person a supply of those aids to beauty which every woman is liable to need at any moment—will doubtless suggest themselves; but I have said more than enough, I think, to give him the right idea.

(It should be remembered, however, that there are certain domestic provinces which the most helpless of wives regards as her very own. An occasional hint *re* the frying of bacon is unlikely to be resented, but a husband who repeatedly elbows the cook aside in order to demonstrate the right way of cooking this or that is apt to find himself cookless—and possibly even wifeless—within a month at the most. Nor should he, if he likes a quiet life, ever presume to criticize his partner's choice of curtains, carpets, or spring hats.)

Anyway, if any young married couple who (or which) faithfully obeys the precepts I have here laid down—if any such young couple (I repeat, taking a new breath) fails to live in perfect amity for at least eleven months, nobody will be less dumbfounded than myself.

And that goes for Mr. Heath Robinson too, I shouldn't wonder.

Compendium

Domestic economy

THE YOUNG IDEA

There is one subject on which everybody, married or still at large, is a self-appointed authority, viz: How To Bring Up Other People's Children. Indeed, from the quantity of clotted advice that is published annually on this theme, one gathers that the only people who do not know how to bring up a child are that child's parents.

Mr. Heath Robinson and I, therefore, have no hesitation in rolling up our sleeves, putting out the cat, and adding our contribution to the heap. After all, we were children ourselves once—and rather charming little chaps, if we may say so; why, it seems but yesterday that we were patted on the head by George IV, who mistook us for a couple of other kids— and there is always the chance that one or more of our

The new pram for troublesome children

suggestions may prove helpful to the young husband who discovers, to his mingled astonishment and alarm, that he has achieved fatherhood. I mean to say, we can't be wrong every time.

Ordinarily the relationship between a novice father and small baby is one of mutual distrust, tinged slightly with concern. To a baby, a father is an amorphous object that looms sheepishly about the place, unjustifiably prodding people in the ribs and making fatuous remarks. To a father, a baby is just an animated uproar that can be trusted to do its vocal best whenever its exhausted parents are snatching a little sleep.

Consequently the average father is inclined to leave the care and upbringing of his very young entirely to their mother, contenting himself with prodding them from time to time and saying "How's the boy?" in the falsely jovial manner he assumes towards his creditors. This is all wrong, in my opinion, as a little fatherly supervision during its earliest years may easily prevent the child from developing into a fraudulent financier, a three-card-trick expert, a person who wears lavender spats, or a Collector of Taxes.

Among British fathers there exists a strong prejudice against pushing perambulators in public. Fearing the derision of the mob, they would rather appear at the office in a wife-chosen tie than take the kid for an airing on Sunday. This is regrettable, for an intelligent father can do much to mould the character of his infant while he is shoving it round the parish. Besides, by taking on this simple task he earns the gratitude of his wife, who is thus set free to go ahead with her knitting, her manufacture of whortleberry jam, or her study of *Only a Fireman's Daughter: or Love in a Lighthouse*.

Furthermore, it gets the child accustomed to its father's face, and vice versa. On the first few outings, maybe, the little one will weep continuously, wondering what it has ever done to deserve the attentions of this trousered horror. Gradually, however, it will become reconciled to its lot, and ultimately, perhaps, even derive a certain quiet amusement from its contemplation of the parental map.

Mention of perambulators reminds me that now and again—but not more than twice in his lifetime, unless he is completely out of luck—a young husband, to the delight of the neighbours and his own bewilderment, becomes the father of triplets and is faced with the alternatives of buying three perambulators—a costly business—or devoting all his spare time for the best years of his life to exercising the children in turn. To meet this contingency, Mr. Heath Robinson has designed, patented, and registered at Fishmongers' Hall the Tripram, here depicted. This is a perambulator in triplicate, artistically fashioned of Spanish walnut and occupying no more space on the road than a smallish charabanc or a biggish hearse.

The Tripram for triplets

The mother's help

With the help of this conveyance the conscientious triplet-owner can simultaneously propel his little treasures round the vicinage and improve his shoving-muscles. He will get looked at rather a lot, no doubt, by policemen on point-duty and the kind of people who cannot meet one baby, let alone three, without chucking it under the chin; but that—unless he has a prominent hole in his sock—should gratify rather than irk him.

While we are on the subject of shoving—well, we are, are we not?—I would commend to the notice of

For keeping a child at her practice

parents the Heath Robinson Rollapram, or Pramrolla. This consists simply of a stout wicker basket attached to a common (or garden) roller, and enables Mummy to curl up cosily with a good book while Daddy combines the functions of a hen-pecked husband with those of a daily gardener. Pretty neat, we think.

The necessity of teaching small children to walk is often overlooked by their immediate ancestors. Instinct, the latter argue, will show the little blighters how. Well, so it will; but a child that walks too often and too soon is liable not only to fall repeatedly on its silly little face, knocking its features sideways, but to grow so bandy about the legs that on attaining manhood it has no choice but to become a jockey, no matter how intense its yearning to be a professional flautist or a

A perfect husband

Inculcating polite habits in the young

salesman of water-softeners. This, inevitably, embitters its outlook on life and makes it brood a good deal.

The contraption here shown has been designed by Mr. Heath Robinson, that many-sided genius, expressly to obviate that risk. The machine itself being as self-explanatory as a machine can be without actually becoming boring, I need only add that the bait can be varied to suit each individual inmate, some children responding more readily to a tomato or a woolly rabbit than to a teething-ring.

So much for the physical aspect of the infant's early education; now for the moral side (don't go away, you

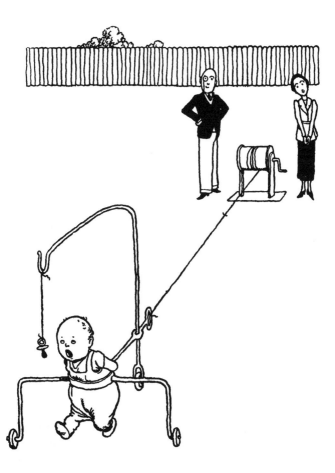

First lessons in walking

boys). It is during its earliest years that such virtues as punctuality, courtesy, good manners, honesty, and thrift should be inculcated in the kid; and who better qualified as an inculcator than the said kid's father? (Unless, of course, he happens to lack all those virtues himself, in which case he must leave it to Mother.)

Table-manners—without a full set of which no adolescent can hope to be invited to tea at the Vicarage—are best taught patiently by personal example, rather than forcibly with the back of a hairbrush. When little Cedric at his first encounter with a sago pudding hurls it violently to the floor—and who can blame him, after all?—the wise father will merely frown reprovingly and fall upon *his* portion with ostentatious gusto, even if he has to go and lie down afterwards in a darkened room. The child thus tacitly rebuked, will feel remorse for the first time in its young life, and thereafter will think twice before refusing even tapioca.

Equitable distribution

A lesson in how it is done

In the same way, any tendency to greed in young children can be checked by the installation on the groaning-board of a small weighing-machine—as used by Society matrons to discover that they are getting stouter all the time—so that the youngsters can see the fodder being accurately apportioned among them, and at the same time—providing Daddy knows anything about the subject, which is unlikely—learn something about calories, proteins, ohms, kilowatts, and other gastronomic oddities.

Parents who are opposed on moral, political, or financial grounds to the purchase of weighing-machines can achieve the same result by reserving all the best victuals for themselves and letting their young subsist as best it can on bowls of gruel, old crusts, the unconsumed portion of last Saturday's blancmange, and similar bric-a-brac. But this method, though guaranteed eventually to cure any child of an Oliver-Twist or more-please complex, seems to me unnecessarily harsh and liable to engender in the infant's mind a sense of frustration that may impel it, when it grows big enough, to kick its father sharply in the pants with the idea of getting its own back. (Not its own pants, of course; the phrase is merely colloquial.)

In the life of every child worthy of the name there are moments when its little metabolism cries out for medicine of one kind or another. The practice, regrettably prevalent among inexperienced parents, of forcing the youthful jaws apart with a tyre-lever and flinging the healing potion down the little gullet has nothing to commend it. As an alternative, the Heath Robinson Physicator (here illustrated) would undoubtedly be warmly approved by the medical fraternity if the latter could be persuaded to return early from golf and look at it.

As the diagram shows, this apparatus can easily be erected in the nursery by any mechanically minded parent at a very reasonable cost, so simple are its ingredients—a few second-hand pulley-wheels, a leg from a disused bedstead, a good deal of string, the in-and-out part of a borrowed concertina, one or two stout nails, and an inexpensive jack-in-the-box, obtainable at any reputable toyshop. With the help of this device,

*Ingenious ruse for administering a dose
of medicine to a boisterous boy*

*Strenuous effort to amuse
a fractious child*

the most nauseous draught can be administered to the most restive child before it (the child, I mean) can cry: "Hey, chuck it!" Even quite elderly persons—ailing financiers, for example, or wholesale florists in the throes of measles—can be successfully physicked in this manner, a model contango in plasticine or a little woolly chrysanthemum being substituted for the jack-in-the-box unless the patient is in his second childhood, as he may very well be.

Neither Mr. Heath Robinson nor I, fearless though we are, would dare to claim that in this chapter we have covered every aspect of the care and maintenance of kids. We feel pretty confident, however, that the young father who cuts out the foregoing pages and pastes them in the lining of his hat—for ready reference—will have only himself to blame if all his offspring develop into duds. Actually, of course, he will blame their mother; but that will be no concern of ours, thank goodness.

Telling the truth

A perfect golfing husband

Morning darts

SPORTS AND HOBBIES

As any experienced psychologist will admit—preferably for a consideration—a hobby of some kind is very useful to those who wish to retain their sense of proportion. And as a sense of proportion is one of the things—others being a cookery-book, a hat-rack, an overdraft, and a pair of egg-spoons—no modern married couple can afford to be without, the wise young husband will ensure that he and the little woman have at least one common interest (not *too* common, however, because these things get about and people talk so) which will give them something other than their respective grievances to discuss at meals.

Hobbies suitable for the newly married are of two main types—the active and the passive. Among the former are such robust pastimes as golf, toxophily, tennis, mountaineering, big-game hunting, skating,

A new instrument for testing Polly's blood pressure

archaeology, and playing the xylophone; the latter include chess, astronomy, fishing, reading banned books, and backing dead certainties which seldom are. Common to both categories is pet-keeping, which can be extremely active (as when the pets concerned are mustangs or performing fleas) or delightfully passive (as when they are pedigree newts).

Many young married people nowadays go in for pets, arguing that they are cheaper than children and no less entertaining. That may well be, but there is no doubt that many couples in danger of drifting apart—owing to his habit of dining without a collar, or her addiction to spring onions—have been re-united at the bowlside of an unwell goldfish, or forgotten their differences in their anxiety at a sudden rise in their parrot's blood pressure. A further advantage of pet-owning is that the wife always has somebody at hand

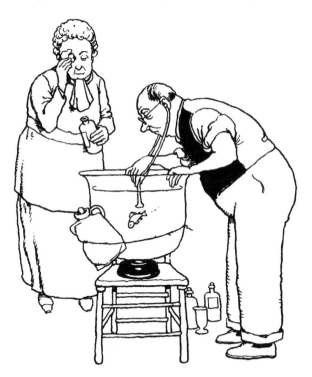

Listening-in to an ailing goldfish

*Practical aeronautics in comfort
for married people*

A useful hobby: breeding plaice

who cannot answer back when she is in one of her moods, while the husband can take it out on the canary, marmoset, or ring-tailed guinea-pig whenever he drops a packet in the City or steps barefoot on a collar-stud.

Among the jollier ways of spending the long winter evenings is pet-keeping for profit. The energetic young wife can always eke out her housekeeping allowance by breeding rabbits, whose wool is greatly in demand among the makers of fur coats. Plaice—harmless and tractable fish, though flattish—are quite easy to rear, and fetch nice prices at Billingsgate. An even more original hobby is the breeding of clothes-moths for sale to importers of moth-balls, who release the insects privily by night in districts where their commodity is not booming at the moment. (Slightly unethical, perhaps, but what fun!)

A mutual interest in art, fishing, archaeology, or parachuting has saved more than one marriage from coming irreparably unstuck. With the help of a "Pair-o-Chute" (see diagram), husband and wife can make enjoyable descents from the stratosphere on Saturday afternoons without interrupting their conversation, tea, or game of picquet. Those who have no head for heights, however, would do better to try fishing, which is an agreeable way of doing nothing and affords a solution of that age-old problem: What the Deuce to do with the Unconsumed Portion of the Wedding-Cake. Not even fish, one imagines, really *like* wedding-cake, but when used as bait it has a certain novelty-value which compensates for its inedibility.

Breeding a fancy strain of the clothes-moth

*How to dispose of what is left over
of the bride's cake*

HOW TO BE A PERFECT HUSBAND

Although the more advanced forms of archaeology, which usually involve repeated visits to Egypt and a good deal of sand in the boots, are too expensive for the average young married couple, it is possible—as the illustration shows—to go through all the necessary motions in the back garden at a very moderate cost. Though the resultant booty will probably not be such as to delight the British Museum, one never knows what will turn up, except that it may be anything from an eighteenth-century salmon-tin to one of the local water-mains. A point to be borne in mind is that things excavated in this way from gardens are seldom attended by a Curse, so that the amateur archaeologist runs little risk of offending the Powers of Darkness and breaking out suddenly in boils. (Unless, of course, he inadvertently punctures the water-main, which is definitely Bad Luck.)

Much of the foregoing applies equally to mountaineering, which cannot be done in a big way without an Alp, a return ticket to Switzerland, and a certain amount of spare time. The side of an ordinary house or block of flats, however, is as hard to climb as any Alp, and far more accessible; and young couples who are keen on that sort of thing can beguile their leisure hours very pleasantly by shinning up and down their premises, having first obtained their landlord's blessing on the enterprise and warned the policeman on the beat to keep away from under.

For those who are opposed both to livestock in the home (on the ground that it upsets the maids and chews holes in the curtains) and to strenuous physical exercise (which does undoubtedly exhaust the tissues and wear out the boots), music is an excellent alternative. Music,

Archaeology in the back garden

Taking the cat's temperature

as every schoolboy knows, is capable of soothing the most savage breast; and the breast of every married couple is apt to get a bit savage at times, what with one thing and another.

At such moments melody is a potent influence for peace, experiments conducted by the Bigger and Brighter Marriage League having shown that it is impossible to quarrel effectively while playing a couple

*Mountaineering as a hobby
in the London Suburbs*

A duet on the trombonium

of kettledrums or rendering Beethoven's "Lament for a Perishing Lizard" on a trombonium. (I beg your pardon? Why, certainly. The trombonium is a married instrument invented by Mr. Heath Robinson in one of his less responsible moments, but none the worse for that. For specifications, see sketch-map.)

Even crooning—which is the art or science (or crime, if you feel that way about it) of emitting clotted noises suggesting the escape of treacle from a bath— can be used to check an incipient bicker that might otherwise develop into target-practice with the tea-things. A young husband's natural impulse, on first hearing his wife croon, is to stun her with a fire-iron; but if he can steel himself to endure the initial agony and consider the broader aspects of the matter he will realize that a crooning woman is a woman temporarily incapable of other mischief, such as exchanging his favourite old trousers for a potted aspidistra, or asking wifely questions about the red-haired girl at the tobacconist's. Thus we see that, as Confucius pointed out, there is no evil without its attendant good.

SPORTS AND HOBBIES

A quiet pastime for the newly married, and one that is less likely to make the neighbours hammer on the party-wall, is the study of the stars. Knowing nothing about astrology, except that persons born under the sign of Saturn have a tendency to web-feet, I cannot say how this is done; but as recreation for two young people of placid tastes and sedentary habits it seems to have much to commend it. After all, the stars are always there, practically as good as new and casting their pale radiance impartially upon the just, the unjust, and even officials of the Inland Revenue Department; all one has to do is to buy a suitable telescope—preferably one of those double models, here depicted, which obviate unseemly jostling at the eyepiece—and look at them. As a recreation for young-marrieds this is

Early morning practice for the crooner

Astronomy for married folk

unquestionably cheaper than golf, less exhausting than tennis, and more instructive than breeding silkworms.

As for Art, this is a helpful and inexpensive hobby for those who like to sit down a good deal and are not actually colour-blind. Nowadays no artistic training is necessary, as paintings of recognizable subjects are condemned as "mere coloured photographs" by the intelligentzia and loudly snorted at. Thus, when painting a cow at play, one should endeavour to portray the rhythmic tone-values inherent in the state of cowship, rather than the animal itself. This, of course, simplifies things a lot, since one man's idea of a rhythmic tone-value is just as good as another's. In fact, modern painting is so easy that a child can do it; and far too many children do, apparently.

To those for whom painting has no allure, owing to the poor facilities it affords for gambling, I would recommend the ingenious game, here shown, which is known as "Spot-the-Ace". This is suitable for any number of players, and can be gambled on to any extent, while the anti-gambling faction can play for cucumbers, boiled sweets, kisses, or even little bits of tape.

Spotting-the-Ace
A new game of patience

93

The thoughtful husband

In conclusion, to those who awake in the morning with a fattish head and a feeling of animosity towards the Universe, may I recommend the game of "Bed-darts", one of the most amusing children of Mr. Heath Robinson's fertile brain? If there is a time when the average married couple needs a little distraction, it is when they have been brutally aroused by the postman's knock (two bulb catalogues, an invitation to support the local Cats' Home, and three letters beginning: "Dear sir, Unless . . .") from dreams of affluence and Tahiti; and a jolly game of darts is just what is needed to loosen up the corpuscles and prepare the mind, if any, to face another day. Why nobody has thought

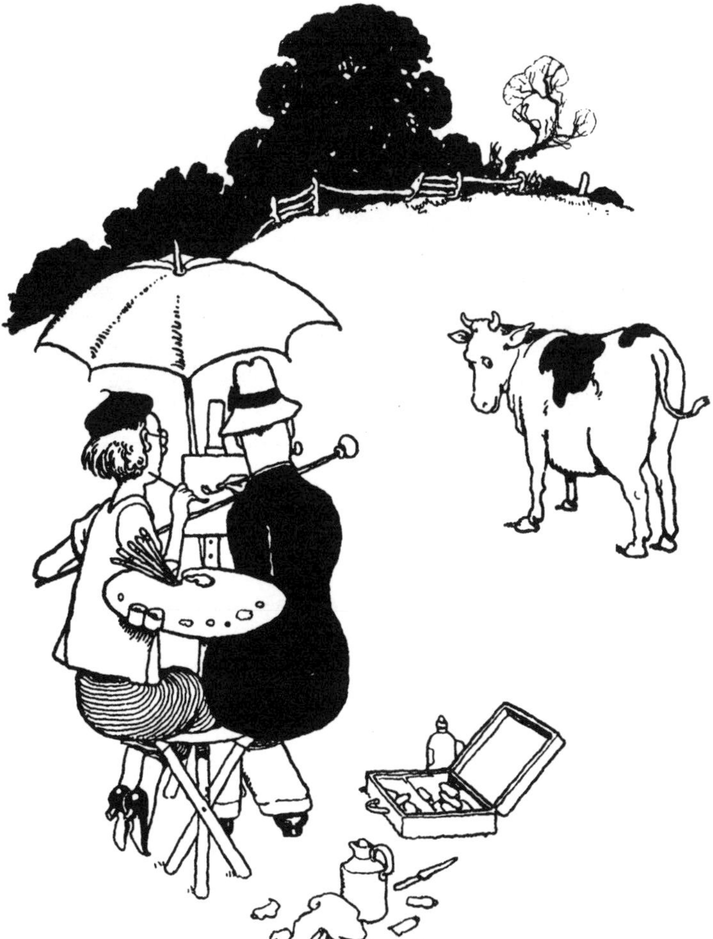

L'art mutuel

How to pass the time on the river when you have forgotten how to row

of this before is one of the things—others being the precise purpose of the Pyramids and the reason why cows get up stern first—I cannot understand.

Well, well! Far be it from me to claim that this chapter covers every angle of this particular question. I feel very strongly, however, that any young married couple who remain completely uninspired by the above painstaking suggestions, and who still cannot imagine what to do with their spare time, would be well advised to have their heads examined by a doctor. And there, if I have anything to do with it, we will let the matter rest.

Taking the goldfish for an airing

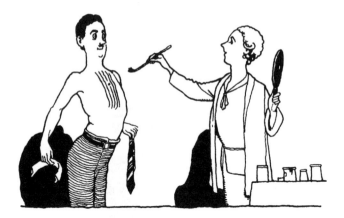

When the shirt does not come home from the wash

DOMESTIC DIFFICULTIES

Since nothing in this imperfect world is perfect—
except asparagus and the south-eastern aspect
of a policewoman by moonlight—little domestic
contretemps of one kind or another are bound
occasionally to occur in even the happiest marriages.
At such moments the conscientious husband will refrain
from flying into a passion and saying things that he will
afterwards regret; rather will he remain collected and
unruffled and bend all his intellect, if any, to bear on the
solution of the difficulty.

The way of a man with a maid has been freely
remarked on by the poets, rather snootily; but the way
of a laundry with its clients' vestments is even more
peculiar. Thus there are times in the life of every British
breadwinner when, his shirts having failed to return from

the wash, he is faced with the alternatives of remaining steadfastly in bed or attending a Shareholders' Meeting in his vest. Actually, however, there is no need on these occasions for any loss of temper or exchange of curt remarks; by keeping perfectly calm and getting the little woman to paint his upper torso in shirt-like stripes of gaily contrasted colours, the breadwinner— first attaching his collar to the back of his neck by a small piece of stamp-paper—can go boldly forth and face the world, secure behind his natty camouflage. (Many business men, indeed, aver that the painted-on shirt is much superior to the ordinary struggled-into variety, in that it can be worn for weeks and never gets frayed at the cuffs; but that, like the exact whereabouts of Atlantis, is a matter of opinion.)

Though coal-fires, thanks to the invention of the common therm and the larger whey-faced kilowatt, are becoming increasingly scarce, a few are still to be found here and there, discharging volumes of nauseous smoke into the room whenever the wind is in the south—or the north, as the case may be, or even the west; or the east, for that matter. As there is nothing more conducive to loss of temper and watering of the eyes than a smoky fire, husbands who are plagued by this nuisance would do well to glance keenly at the appended sketch of the Heath Robinson Smokeliminator—or "Daisy", as it is familiarly termed in the trade.

This consists of a large metal shield—originally a dustbin-lid or purloined manhole-cover, if the truth were known—suspended by stout clamps from the mantelshelf and connected with the Great Outdoors by a length of home-made stove-pipe. Utterly baffled by this device, the smoke has no choice but to exit

A neat way of dealing with a smoky chimney

disgruntled through the window, leaving the air of the parlour unpolluted and giving officious neighbours a chance to ring up the Fire Brigade. If this neat contraption has a fault—which, mark you, neither I nor Mr. Heath Robinson nor the Gas, Light, and Coke Company are prepared to admit—it is that it excludes not only all smoke from the room, but most of the fire as well. Thicker underwear, however, or a small auxiliary oil-stove will remedy *that* little fault.

Somewhat similar in general construction is the Heath Robinson "Anticroon" Self-Isolater, here shown. In every normal British household there are two distinct

When the kitchen chimney catches fire

*Maintaining a Guy Fawkes bonfire
under difficulties*

schools of thought—those who regard radio as the greatest invention since the corkscrew, and those who prefer spinach. Each faction has its point of view, the one arguing that life without the Fat Stock Prices is just an arid desert, and the other maintaining that to be brayed at by sopranos when one is trying to read the "Hairdressers' Quarterly" is an experience to exasperate the mildest.

In the past this difference of opinion has caused many a once-happy couple to part and go their separate ways, muttering under their breath. Hence the Self-Isolater, which can be had in various sizes and is fitted with eye-pieces, pipe-aperture, Yale lock, smoke-escape-valve and decorative cretonne lining. Safe within this din-proof sanctuary, the husband who

When you want a quiet read in the evening

prefers silence to adenoidal song can concentrate with a calm mind and an unbludgeoned ear upon anything from *Bradshaw's Railway Guide* to the *Report of the Commission of Inquiry into the Prevalence of Ambidextrous Vegetarians in the Wholesale Tricycle Industry.*

It is generally agreed, I think, that one of the most potent causes of unrest in the home is the tendency of collar-studs to slip down the backs of shirts. A man whose stud has played him this characteristically dirty trick is in an unenviable position, since to retrieve the thing he must either strip to the buff again—thereby, very likely, missing his train and getting in bad with his boss—or tie himself into knots that only a sailor could unravel; nor, if he is of a ticklish temperament, can he enlist his wife to do the retrieving for him, save at the risk of death by laughter.

Meditating on this problem in his bath, in his favourite balloon, while waiting for trains, and elsewhere, Mr. Heath Robinson has evolved an apparatus which finally disposes of this difficulty. This gadget is so simple as to be almost half-witted, its chief components being a football, a ten-pound weight, a Homburg hat, some rubber tubing, and a modicum of string. On the machine being set in action, as the diagram makes plain, a powerful current of air is forced up the patient's trousers, thus dislodging the truant stud, which is instantly trapped by the lurking Homburg (for which a bowler or pith-helmet may be substituted, if desired). For ingenuity of design and infallibility in action, this inexpensive doohickus is worthy to rank, in my opinion, with the typewriter, the alarm-clock, and the tripartite interlocutory Weltschmerz engine which inserts the dents in dog-biscuits.

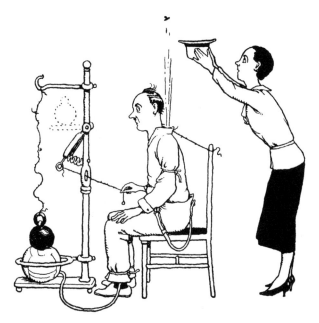

*A neat contraption for recovering a collar-stud
which has slipped down the back*

While we are discussing machinery, I would like to draw the attention of all except incurable wasp-lovers to Mr. Heath Robinson's Mobile Wasp-Gun, which is guaranteed to make the most bellicose wasp wish that its parents had been water-voles or wart-hogs. With the help of this grim weapon—which should not be operated without boxing-gloves—the husband whose wife tends to come over all queer at the sight of a wasp can abolish the insect and a good deal of the lighter

When the flannel bags have shrunk in the wash

furniture in approximately two minutes. The Wasp-Gun, it seems to me, is what keen sportsmen of all ages have been awaiting without knowing it, and should command a steady sale among those who have been compelled by advancing years or increasing corpulence to give up their partridge-shooting.

The husband who wishes to make life one grand, sweet song for his little old ball-and-chain will be at pains to keep his temper, not only in such major crises as I have touched upon, but also in those moments of lesser irritation which inevitably crop up now and then. A man's natural impulse, for example, on discovering, when sunk to his glottis in the bath, that there is no

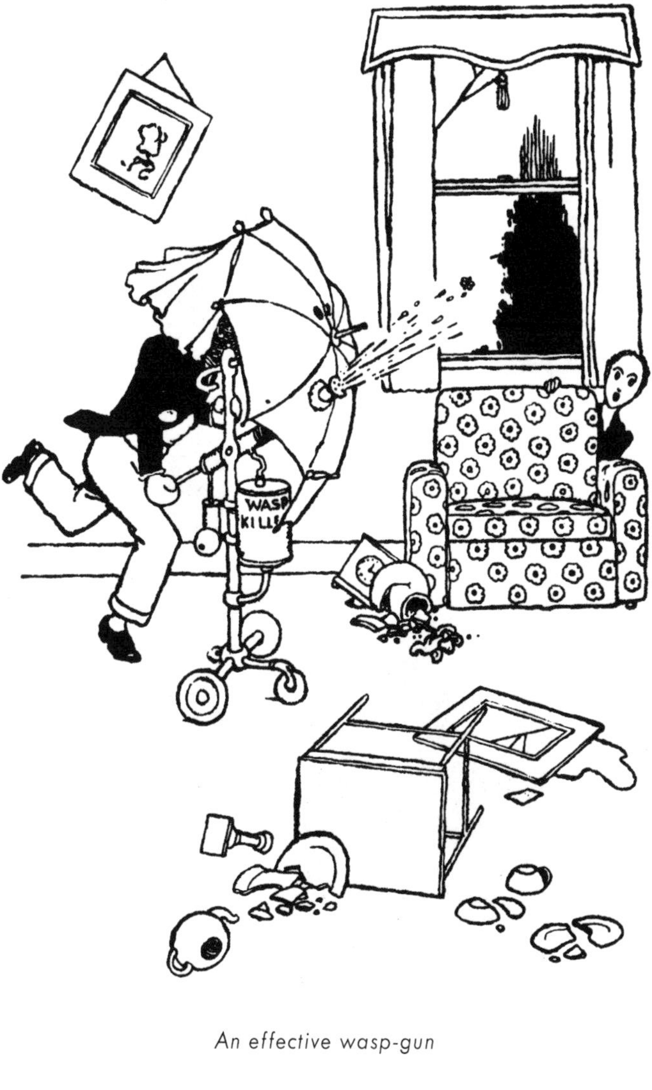
WASP
KILLE

An effective wasp-gun

Signalling no soap in the bathroom

soap available, is to vent his annoyance in a bull-like bellow upon the nearest maid, wife, or member of the family. But the thoughtful husband, reflecting that the best of wives is prone to occasional error, will utter no raucous lamentations, but by signalling quietly from the bathroom window with a towel or his little woolly pants, will apprise the passers-by of his predicament and so ensure that the sad news is broken to his wife in a seemly and decorous manner.

In the same way, when his eagerly awaited break-fast-egg proves to be slightly cold, he will not cast it from him with a vicious oath and stamp madly from the room, leaving the little woman weeping into the toast-rack. On the contrary, he will treat the matter as a merry jest and encourage the l.w. to express her sympathy and contrition by re-warming the egg by match-power.

The cold egg

Though every wife likes to mother her husband a bit, she is liable to turn peevish if she is constantly called upon to singe his hair, pick up his fallen brace-buttons, or perform similar little chores which he could easily do for himself. If he *must* singe his hair, let him do it single-handed, in the manner here shown. As for brace-buttons, the tendency of these to fly off is admittedly irritating; but on such occasions there is no need to cry out and beat the breast. By simply looping the braces over the skull (see diagram) the trousers can be held *in situ* until Madam has finished the batter-pudding and can attend to the matter.

For singeing the hair at the back of the head

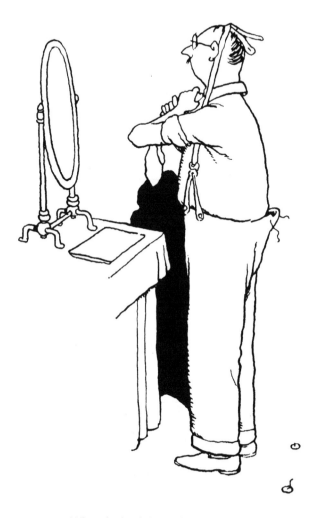

When the back brace-buttons fall off

An awkward predicament—

—and an artistic way out of it

In conclusion—and about time too—a tip for husbands who spill ink, as the majority of husbands do at least once on their long journey from the altar to the grave. Nothing looks worse than a solitary inkstain on a table-cloth; but a lot of ink-stains, similar in shape and artistically distributed, are what a table-cloth can hardly fail to be improved in appearance by. *Verb sap* (if that means what I hope it does).

How to brush the back of your coat without troubling your wife

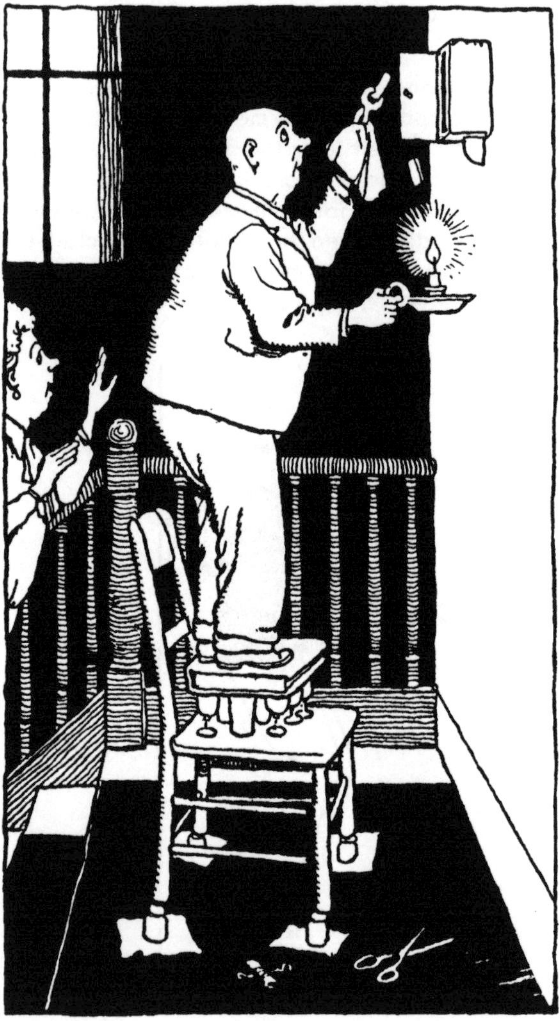

Replacing a fuse

DOMESTIC DIFFICULTIES

Well, there we are. As the old adage puts it:

**It's the little things that count, it's the little
    things that matter.
It's the little things that send a guy more
    cuckoo than a hatter.**

By committing this simple verse to memory, and
by reading the foregoing chapter twice daily after
meals, the husband who aspires to a serene married
life, undisturbed by tiffs, bickers, sulks, or blows from
an umbrella, will put himself well on the way towards
achieving that praiseworthy end.

More than that, this being Early Closing Day, I
really cannot say.

Training a child to avoid greed

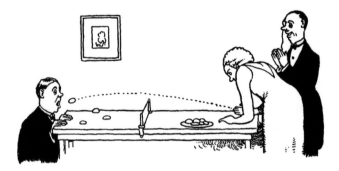

The indoor game of Shovaroon

MIDDLE AGE AND HOW TO MEET IT

On or about his forty-third birthday the average husband is apt to realize—probably when he is running vainly for a bus or being soundly beaten at tennis by his niece from Roedean—that he is no longer so young as he was. Two courses are then open to him. He can (a) go all morose and broody and let himself degenerate gradually into an elderly bore of the egg-shaped type that sits about in the most comfortable arm-chair, breathing heavily and lamenting the Good Old Days, or he can (b) face the situation philosophically and cast about for some method of getting a little fun out of his middle age.

For the husband who wishes to retain the esteem and affection of his wife, the second course is manifestly the wiser. For the said wife is not getting any younger, either, and a husband whose appearance and demeanour constantly remind her of that fact is likely to get on her nerves a bit.

A mistake made by many men on reaching middle age is that of letting themselves spread in all directions, thus becoming pear-shaped. Though no man of mature years can hope to recapture That Schoolboy Figure which was once his pride and joy, he owes it to his self-respect to keep his perimeter within reasonable bounds, either by physical exercise or by some such device as the Heath Robinson Self-Dwindler (see diagram). This inexpensive gadget, which can be attached to any kitchen table, is fitted with a reliable weight-gauge, a mahogany tray for light refreshments and several detachable twelve-pound weights, so that the customer can adjust the pressure on his abdomen to

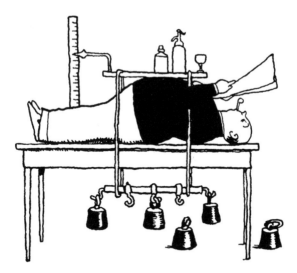

For preserving the figure and checking the onslaught of Anno Domini in comfort

the point where it is guaranteed to flatten him, slowly but surely, without giving him a pain in the neck or elsewhere. This machine—leaving as it does the hands free for juggling, needlework, or the manipulation of Blue Books—is particularly suitable for Cabinet Ministers, translators of Arabian poetry, and others who do not earn their living with their feet.

A certain amount of physical exercise, of course, is necessary to those who wish to avoid the kind of corpulence that is giggled at in trams. Nor, just because he will never see forty again—or thirty, for that matter—need the conscientious husband shun all those sports which he enjoyed when he and the world were young. If, for example, he finds ordinary cricket too strenuous for his ageing bones, he can adapt it to his needs in the manner illustrated, provided he can assemble twenty-one others of similar age, shape, and inclinations. Played in arm-chairs and with a ball of sponge, the game hardens no arteries, causes no painful contusions, and is not noticeably slower than a normal Test Match.

Another good game for those who have outgrown their marbles and lost their aptitude for hopscotch is bowls, which is a sort of cueless billiards, played under the vault of Heaven. I am a little doubtful about Mr. Heath Robinson's hint to the bowlster whose stooping days are over, for large circular excavations do no lasting good to the average bowling-green. Still, there is no harm in trying, is there?

Yes, but—I hear the lady in black bombazine and the bonnet with bugles demanding—what about the wife, hey? Middle-aged though she may be, is *she* to have no fun and games? While her spouse roysters on

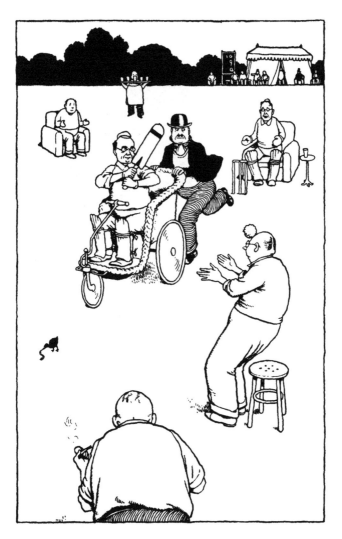

Cricket for the middle-aged

To avoid stooping at bowls

the cricket-lawn or bowl-pitch, must she sit solitary at home, with only her tatting to keep her mind off the high cost of cutlets and the tendency of children to grow through their little socks?

Have patience, lady. I am about to expound, in a profusely illustrated manner, various ways in which a wife who has graduated from the debutante class can split a little relaxation with her good man—as we will call him laughingly, having no evidence to the contrary. Mr. Heath Robinson, indeed, has even gone so far as to invent a very jolly game, provisionally registered with the Jockey Club as "Hunt-The-Seltzer", expressly for middle-aged couples and their friends.

"Hunt-The-Seltzer"—a vigorous game
for water diviners

Giving the wife a chance

Most people number at least one water-diviner among their acquaintances; and since a person who can divine water can presumably divine soda-water, too, a dozen siphons and a few fathoms of stout twine are all that is needed to ensure that an enjoyable and invigorating time is had by all. The game can be arranged for any number of players, and any siphons that fail to explode during the merry romp can be used at the subsequent thirst-quenching.

Although lawn-tennis of the Wimbledon or where-did-that-one-go brand is a trifle too arduous for those who can remember the halcyon days when beer was twopence a pint, a modified form of the game can still be enjoyed by the middle-aged. As a means of keeping a wife out of the local milliner's and doing the husband's corpuscles a bit of lasting good, a daily singles in the garden is both cheap and effective. If, as is often the case, the little woman—owing to her inferior physique, or her corns, or something—is no match for her life's partner, the latter can easily adjust the matter by removing the strings from his racket. This adds considerably to the excitement of the game, and is a dodge that might well be adopted in the Davis Cup contests, in my opinion.

As the weather in these tight little islands is not invariably (or even often) clement, Mr. Heath Robinson and I, tireless in our zeal, have evolved an indoor game—to be known, if nobody has any objection, as "Shovaroon", the first "o" on the left being pronounced as the "u" in "gumboil"—which is the very thing for married couples whose mutual stock of conversation was exhausted years ago.

A home-made Japanese fiddle

This, as the illustration shows, is a cross between ping-pong, afternoon tea, and shove-halfpenny, and is a good way of utilizing those old macaroons which accumulate in the most orderly households. "Shovaroon" calls for a considerable amount of skill, points being awarded as follows:

Direct hit in mouth	·	·	5	points
„ „ on left eye	·	·	2	„
„ „ on right eye	·	·	2	„
„ „ on nose	·	·	3	„
Teeth dislodged	·	·	1	point per tooth

The first player to score 50 is adjudged the winner, and may be rewarded with anything from a book of stamps to a small wooden model of Stonehenge.

A common love of music—not to be confused with a love of common music—has helped many a married pair to survive their middle age. There is no prettier sight, to my mind, than a husband and wife beguiling the afternoon of their days with the aid of a piano, a concertina, a triangle, or a double-handed Swedish nose-flute. Even those who cannot afford so much as a second-hand mouth-organ need not deny themselves the joys of melody, as it is a simple matter to construct a Japanese fiddle from the flotsam to be found in every scullery, or to convert a super-annuated vacuum-cleaner into a poor relation of the bagpipes.

Well, that, I think, is about all—why, rip me and sink me and cram me with whelks, I almost forget to mention the Heath Robinson Breakfast-Bulwark! This, though

For the prevention of breakfast-time acerbities

so far-reaching in its effect, is simply a cherrywood screen, designed to stand vertically on the breakfast-table and fitted with an orifice through which mugs of tea, pieces of cold ham, and portions of *sole frite sur le pont d' Avignon* can be freely bandied back and forth. To people who have been married for years this dingus should have a powerful appeal, as it relieves

126

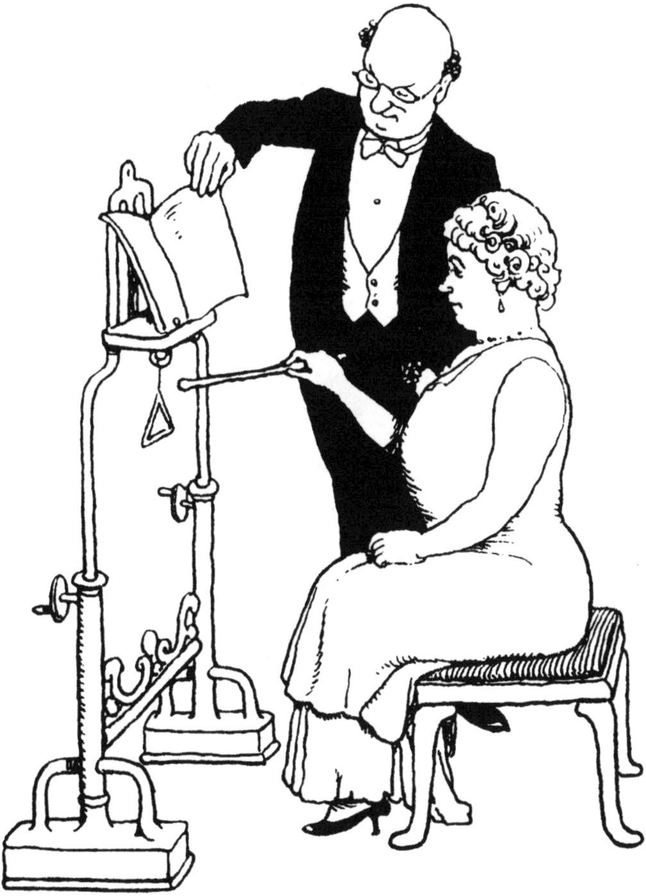

A solo on the triangle

the husband of the necessity of contemplating his wife, and vice versa, at a time of day when neither is feeling sociable or even mildly matey.

The thanks of all such will, I am sure, go out to Mr. Heath Robinson for conceiving this veritable boon. Men have won medals for less, if you ask me.

The Vacuophone

Washing day

CONCLUSION

The reader (if he or she is still awake) may think it rather presumptuous of Mr. Heath Robinson and myself to attempt to deal with so large a subject in so small a volume. But it is impossible, in less than some 500,000 words—which, frankly, is more than I and Mr. Heath Robinson know between us—to cover *every* angle of the married state, or to mention *every* problem that may confront the modern husband on his slow but steady progress from the altar to the almshouse. The modest dimensions of this work, therefore, are due not so much to our natural indolence as to a definite design.

Our aim has been merely to suggest a general line of conduct that should give pretty good results and to provide the about-to-be married with a handy textbook that can be carried in the pocket (or in the crown of the hat, if preferred), and consulted at any convenient moment. The broader issues, in short, are all that we have tried to touch upon; the novice husband who craves advice about such minor tribulations as the ties his wife gives him at Christmas must just worry it out for himself and act as his conscience dictates. And, if he has thoroughly studied this little book, he won't go far wrong, bless his heart!

Well, that concludes the business of the evening—and about time, too, as the lady in black bombazine and the bonnet with bugles very justly remarks. It only remains to add that if, as a result of the publication of this little masterpiece, Britain's divorce-rate declines by about fifty per cent during the next few years, Mr. Heath Robinson ("Towser" to me, by the way) and I will be deeply gratified.

And pretty astonished, too, we don't mind admitting.

THE END

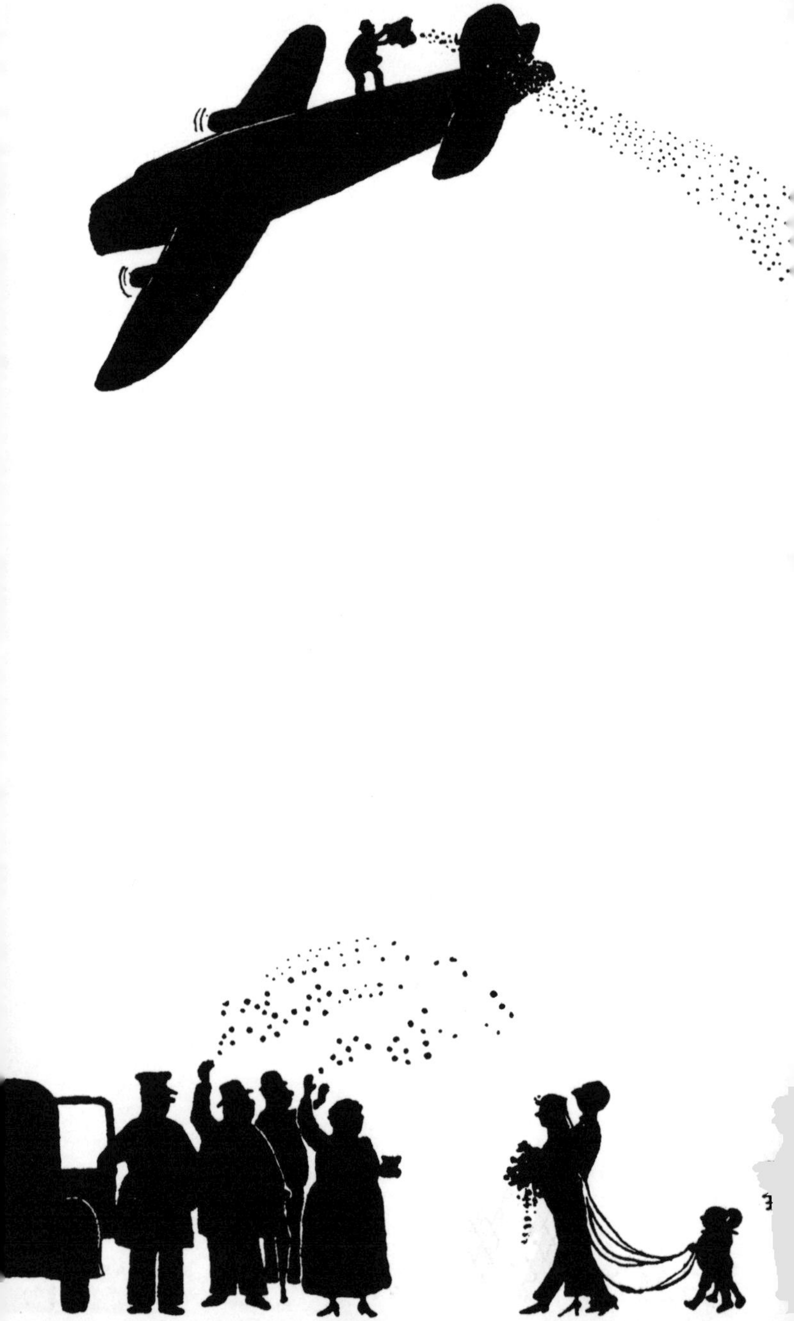